I0114729

NIGERIA WITHOUT NIGERIANS?

BOKO HARAM AND THE CRISIS IN NIGERIA'S NATION-BUILDING PROJECT

Published by

Adonis & Abbey Publishers Ltd
P.O. Box 43418
London
SE11 4XZ
Tel: + 44 845 388 7248
Website: http://www.adonis-abbey.com
Email: editor@adonis-abbey.com

Nigeria
Adonis & Abbey Publishing Company
P.O. Box 10546 Abuja,
Nigeria
Tel: +234 816 5970458

First Edition, August 2012

Copyright 2012 © Jideofor Adibe

British Library Cataloguing-in-Publication Data
A catalogue record for this book is available from the British
Library

ISBN: 978-1-909112-02-5

The moral right of the author has been asserted All rights
reserved. No part of this book may be reproduced, stored in a
retrieval system or transmitted at any time or by any means
without the prior permission of the publisher
Printed and bound in Great Britain

NIGERIA WITHOUT NIGERIANS?

BOKO HARAM AND THE CRISIS IN NIGERIA'S NATION-BUILDING

Adonis & Abbey
Publishers Ltd

Table of Contents

Preface
....vii

Chapter 1
Introduction: Nigeria and the making of a nation-state
....11

Chapter 2
Boko Haram: Evolution and Radicalization
....29

Chapter 3
Explaining the Boko Haram phenomenon
....45

Chapter 4
Crisis in Nigeria's Nation-Building Project
....83

Chapter 5
Conclusions and recommendations
....105

Index
....127
.

Dedication

For my late mother: Mrs Patricia Adibe.

And children:

Adaobi, Udoka and Didi.

With all my love

Preface

This monograph arose from a well-received lecture I gave at the Institute for Security Studies; Pretoria, South Africa on February 2 2012 entitled 'Boko Haram as a symptom of the crisis in Nigeria's nation-building'. After the South Africa lecture, I did a three-part serialization of the presentation in my weekly column in the *Daily Trust*. Readers' responses encouraged me to revise the work and publish it as a monograph.

I am grateful to the Institute for Security Studies, Pretoria, South Africa, for the invitation to give the lecture. I am especially grateful to my friends Dr Issaka Souare and Martin Ewi for the warmth and hospitality they accorded me throughout my stay in the Rainbow nation. I am also appreciative of the comments not only of those who attended the lecture in South Africa but also from readers of my column in the *Daily Trust*, especially those who offered comments or provided new insights into the Boko Haram phenomenon.

Some of the ideas in both the original paper presented at ISS and in this monograph were, at various times, bounced off on friends, colleagues and my postgraduate students at the Department of Political Science, Nasarawa State University, Keffi. Their comments have been most valuable in shaping my perspective on the subject.

I am grateful to my colleagues at Nasarawa State University - the Dean of the Faculty of Social sciences, Professor S. A. Ibrahim, the Head of Department of Political Science Dr A.S. Modibbo and colleagues Dr Abullahi Yammah, Dr Yahaya Adadu, and Usman Abu Tom for their support and understanding. I am also most grateful to my PA Alexander Akoje for his tireless contributions.
While the work has benefitted from inputs from various sources, any error of facts or interpretation remains mine and is deeply regretted.

Jideofor Adibe, August 2012

CHAPTER 1

INTRODUCTION:

NIGERIA AND THE MAKING OF A NATION-STATE

One of the aftermaths of the Berlin Conference of 1884-1885 where the European conferees enunciated the principle of 'dual mandate' - that the interest of both Europe and Africa would be best served by maintaining free access to Africa for trade and in turn providing the continent with the benefits of 'European civilization', was that Britain's claims to a sphere of influence in the Niger Basin were acknowledged formally.

The stipulation that only effective occupation would secure full international recognition hastened the establishment of effective British occupation and the creation of protectorates in northern and southern Nigeria. Frederick Lugard, who became High Commissioner for the Protectorate of

Northern Nigeria in 1900, was essentially occupied with transforming the commercial sphere of influence he inherited from the Royal Niger Company (a mercantile company chartered by the British government in the nineteenth century, which formed the basis of the modern state of Nigeria) into a viable territorial unit under effective British political control. He adopted a policy of Indirect Rule, which meant governing the protectorate through traditional authority structures.

In the same 1900 the British Protectorate of Southern Nigeria was formed from a union of the Niger Coast Protectorate (established originally as the Oil Rivers Protectorate in 1891) with territories chartered by the Royal Niger Company below Lokoja on the Niger River. In 1906, the Lagos Colony was added and the territory became officially renamed the Colony and Protectorate of Southern Nigeria.

Some commentators have noted that the unification of the Northern Protectorate and

Protectorate of Southern Nigeria was motivated more by economic reasons than any desire to create a nation-state from the 'marriage of convenience' contrived for the disparate nationalities that were brought together under the new arrangement. Barkan et al (2001) for instance argued that the unification happened basically because the Northern Nigeria Protectorate had a budget deficit which the colonial authorities sought to offset with the budget surpluses from Southern Nigeria. Whatever may be the motive for the unification of 1914, at independence in 1960, the country began to grapple not only with the challenges of governance but also with that of nation-building.

Nation, Nation-State and Nation-building

What is a nation? And what does nation-building entail? There is no commonly accepted definition of these concepts. A 'nation' can be defined as a community of people who share the same or similar cultural heritage such as common language, culture, ethnicity, descent, or history. Conceptualizing a 'nation' in this way however does not recognize separate territoriality as a necessary condition for nationhood. This may probably explain why some Nigerian politicians often suffix nationhood to their ethnicity such as when they talk about the 'Yoruba nation', 'Igbo nation' etc. It is perhaps another way of emphasizing their uniqueness, separateness or even superiority to the other ethnic groups that make up the country. We will consider this notion of nationhood too narrow and too limiting for the purposes of this monograph.

For our purpose, we will use 'nation' to refer to a community or communities of people who share a common territory and government and feel that they are one or ought to be one. In this sense 'nations' are, as Benedict Anderson (1983) would put it 'imagined communities'. For Anderson, a nation is a community socially constructed and imagined by the people who perceive themselves as part of the group. For him, a nation "is imagined because the members of even the smallest nation will never know

14

most of their fellow-members, meet them, or even hear of them, yet in the minds of each lives the image of their communion" (1983:224).

A nation can be distinguished from a State or country which is merely a political and geopolitical entity while a nation embodies the notion of shared ethos, values and norms – hence in Anderson's sense an 'imagined community'. When the two boundaries of 'nation' and 'state' are coterminous, it is often called nation-state. It could be argued that many of the countries in Africa, which are all the creations of colonialism, are 'state-nations' in that previously independent 'nations' (in the sense of a communities sharing a common cultural heritage) where aggregated together into the newly colonially constructed contraptions.

Though making a nation out of the disparate nationalities that make up a colonially constructed country might not have been one of the goals of the colonial masters, it became obvious that for the new countries to succeed, they have to consciously create a sense of community among the previously independent entities that make up the new country. This is where the notion of nation-building comes into play. It is no coincidence that the concept gained currency in the 1950s and 1960s when most of the African countries were either agitating for their independence or had just secured independence from their former colonial masters.

Though there is no unanimity among scholars on the meaning of nation-building, it was primarily used to describe the processes of using state mechanisms to structure a national identity and unity among the diverse communities that make up the colonially constructed countries. For Elaigwu (2005:62), nation-building is a "process by which members of a State create a political community out of an existing political framework". Implicit in this definition is that the peoples in a state could also lead the processes of fashioning a nation from the disparate communities that make up a state-nation. Elaigwu does not imply that the

State's role in the political engineering that will create a 'nation' is subordinate to the role of the peoples in that regard. Rather he seems to suggest that both the State and the peoples in the State have almost equal role to play in nation-building, hence he identified two dimensions of nation-building – vertical and horizontal. As he puts it (2005:62):

> Nation-building involves, on the horizontal plane, the widening of the horizons of identity of the individual or group to include other individuals and/or groups in the state as equal members of the political community entitled to a share of the bitter or the sweet of the system. On the vertical dimension, nation-building entails the identification with the central authority of the state as the symbol of the political community

While we agree that nation-building also takes place on a horizontal plain – i.e. among the different people that make up the different aggregated communities in a country, our focus will be on nation-building as a conscious effort to use state power to forge unity and create an imagined community among the different nationalities that make up a mere geographical expression coined by colonialism to refer to a particular area of influence.

Nation-building is sometimes confused with 'state-building' which merely denotes efforts at strengthening the institutions of a State. Since the creation of the Nigeria State, several efforts have been made to use the mechanisms of state power to fashion out unity among the various ethnicities and communities that were lumped together into the new country. Some of the measures include:

Adoption of a federal constitution

Nigerians embraced federalism as a way for fashioning out 'unity in diversity' and managing the inevitable conflicts that result from the interaction of previously autonomous entities that were brought together into one state by the colonial order. In fact even before independence in 1960, the unitary colonial state had seen itself gradually federalized especially under the Lyttleton Constitution. As Elaigwu (2005:1) explained:

Federalism is essentially a compromise solution in a multinational state between two types of self-determination – the determination provided by a national government which guarantees security for all in the nation-state on the one hand and the self determination of component groups to retain their individual identities on the other hand. .

It is in K.C Wheare's (1964:10) classical formulation, a "method of sharing power so that the general and regional governments are each, within a sphere, co-ordinate and independent". The character of Nigeria's federalism has however varied – from the First Republic where the country was more of a confederation or very loose federalism to the period of military rule where it was essentially unitarism in federal clothing to the present situation where there is an overwhelming dependence of most States on the centre for their survival.

Reflection of Federal Character

It is generally thought that the phrase 'Reflection of Federal Character' was first used by the late General Murtala

Mohammed in his address to the opening session of the Constitution Drafting Committee (CDC) on October 18 1975. In its report, the CDC referred to the country's 'federal character' as the distinctive desire of the peoples of Nigeria to promote national unity, foster national loyalty and give every citizen of Nigeria a sense of belonging to the nation notwithstanding the diversities of ethnic origin, culture, language or religion which may exist and which it is their desire to nourish, harness to the enrichment of the Federal Republic of Nigeria. Section 14 (3) of the 1979 Constitution stated:

> The composition of the Government of the Federation or any of its agencies and the conduct of its affairs shall be carried out in such a manner as to reflect the federal character of Nigeria and the need to promote national unity, and also to command national loyalty, thereby ensuring that there shall be no predominance of persons from a few States or from a few ethnic or other sectional groups in that Government or any of its agencies. (cited in Ammani, no date)

The 50 'wise-men' who drafted the 1979 Constitution justified the entrenchment of the federal character principle in these words:

> "There had in the past been inter-ethnic rivalry to secure the domination of government by one ethnic group or combination of ethnic groups to the exclusion of others. It is therefore essential to have some provision to ensure that the predominance of persons from a few States or from a few ethnic or other sectional groups is avoided in the composition of government, in the appointment or election of persons to high offices in the state (cited in Ammani, no date)

In Nigeria-speak, the 'Federal Character provision of the 1979 Constitution, which was also adopted by subsequent Constitutions, including the current 1999 Constitution, is meant to give every unit of the federation the proverbial 'sense of belonging' and ensure that no unit is marginalized. In fact in 1996, a Federal Character Commission was established via Act No. 34 "to implement and enforce the Federal Character Principle of fairness and equity in the distribution of public posts and socio-economic infrastructures among the various federating units of the Federal Republic of Nigeria.

The provisions of the 1999 Constitution in Sections 14 and 153 consolidated the establishment of the FCC for operation in a democratic system of Government" (Federal Character Commission, no date).

NYSC

The National Youth Service Corp scheme was set up in 1973 to further the goal of building unity in diversity. The scheme made it mandatory for graduates from universities and other institutions of higher learning who are under the age of thirty to serve their nation for one year in states other than their own. The scheme complemented the creation of Federal Government Colleges where bright and promising young pupils are posted to federal schools outside of their home states. In its early years, when there was

22

full employment in the country and some parts of the country had serious shortages of critical skills, the NYSC scheme contributed in filling the skills gap, especially in the area of teaching.

Creation of States

Nigerians have embraced state creation as part of its goal of promoting unity in diversity. The initial impetus for the agitation for the creation of states was largely predicated on fears by ethnic minorities of being dominated by the majority ethnic group or groups in their region. The country has consequently moved from three regions to four regions in 1963; to 12 states in 1967; 19 states in 1976; 21 states in 1987; 30 states in 1991 and 36 in 1996.

Despite these balkanisation and the fact that most of the states depend on the Federation Account to pay even their wage bill, the demand for the creation of more states has continued unabated.

Zoning

Alexis Tocqueville, the French political thinker and historian, developed the phrase 'tyranny of the majority' in his treatise on possible threats to representative democracy in America, including the tendency for democracy to degenerate into 'soft despotism' and 'tyranny of the majority'.

Since Tocqueville, representative or liberal democracy has come a long way, with different political states developing policies to prevent their system from being corrupted into a 'tyranny of the majority'. The notion of human rights, which is necessarily anti-majoritarian in principle and which is vigorously protected and defended in many mature democracies, is one such safeguard. In other political states, where the basis of statehood remains contested or where the state is made up of an agglomeration of different ethnic nationalities, the notion of 'concurrent majority'- in which great decisions are not arrived at through numerical majorities but often require agreement or

24

acceptance by the major interests in the society – is quite popular. In such political states, contrivances like 'government of national unity', the need to reflect the 'federal character' of a country in appointments and 'zoning' are often popular political vocabularies.

The concept of zoning was introduced into Nigeria's political vocabulary by the defunct National Party of Nigeria in 1979 and was embraced by the PDP in 1999. As I argued elsewhere (Adibe, 2010, 2011), zoning, if applied creatively could help to remove the fear of majority tyranny. For instance one of the common complaints, especially by people from the Southern part of the country, is the domination of the North in the country's politics. This charge is not totally unfounded. Statistically, the Yorubas have held the executive presidency of the country for 12 years (between Obasanjo in his military and civilians incarnations and Shonekan as head of Interim Government); the political North for 37 years, the South South since February 11 2010 when Jonathan became the Acting President of the country following Yaradua's incapacitation and the Igbos for about six months (under Ironsi). Although this domination is essentially through military coups and counter coups, it was feared that given the role of ethnicity and religion in Nigerian politics, the North, with its population, number of States and local governments, might continue its domination in a democratic dispensation. This was perhaps one of the immediate reasons why the defunct NPN came up with the idea of 'zoning' in the Second Republic. In essence it was believed that zoning could facilitate the country's journey to real nationhood by assuring every group that they have a realistic chance of producing key political officers of the country.

We shall show later that these efforts at conscious nation-building have not only stalled but have become enmeshed in crisis, which in turn has created a whole array of problems including a rapid de-Nigerianisation process. Our argument is that as people become alienated from the Nigeria project,

26

they seek to negotiate meaning for their existence in primordial identities that often see the state as the cause of their alienation, hence an enemy and a legitimate target. Boko Haram, in our view, is one of the primordial identities into which some people have withdrawn to consequent upon a rapid de-Nigerianisation process.

References

Adibe, Jideofor (2011): 'Zoning: The Fire Next Time', May 11, *Daily Trust* (back page).

Adibe, Jideofor (2010): 'Between majority tyranny, democratic space and PDP's zoning', October 27 Daily Trust, (back page).

Ammani, Aliyu, A. (no date): 'Federal Character Principle as a Necessary Evil', http://www.gamji.com/article8000/NEWS860 3.htm (Accessed July 20, 2012)

Anderson, Benedict (1983): *Imagined Communities: Reflections on the Origin and Spread of Nationalism* (New edition, Brooklyn, Verso),

Barkan, Joel D.; Gboyega, Alex; Stevens, Mike (2001): "State and Local Governance in Nigeria" Public *Sector and Capacity Building Program: Africa Region, World Bank*, http://info.worldbank.org/etools/docs/library/5783/State_and_Governance_Nigeria.htm, August 2, (Accessed July 24, 2012)

Elaigwu, Isawa J (2005): *The Politics of Federalism* (Jos, AHA Publishing House)

Federal Character Commission (no date): 'Establishment of the Federal Character Commission' http://federalcharacter.gov.ng/ (Accessed July 20, 2012)

Wheare K.C. (1964): *Federal Government* (New York, Oxford University Press, Fourth edition)

CHAPTER 2

BOKO HARAM: EVOLUTION AND RADICALISATION

Boko Haram has increasingly become synonymous with insecurity in Nigeria since 2009 when the government launched a clampdown on the group which resulted in some 800 deaths, mostly of the sect members (Adibe, 2012a, 2012b). Mohamed Yusuf, the group's leader was killed in that attack while in police custody.

In what was apparently retaliation for the extra judicial killing of its leader, the group carried out its first terrorist attack in Borno in January 2010 at Dala Alemderi Ward in Maiduguri metropolis which resulted in the death of four people (Vanguard, online, December 10 2011). Since then the sect has intensified its terrorist activities. On June 16 2011 for instance, it bombed the Police Force headquarters in what was thought to be the first case of using a suicide bomber to carry out terrorist activity in Nigeria. On August 26 2012 another suicide bomber blew up the UN headquarters in Abuja, leaving at least 21 people dead and dozens more injured. On January 20 it attacked Kano, leaving more than 185 people dead. In fact, a day hardly passes without news of attacks by the sect. The government has also intensified its military action against the sect, capturing some of its leaders.

Name

Members of the sect popularly known as Boko Haram prefer to be known by their Arabic name - *Jama'atu Ahlis Sunna Lidda'awati Wal-Jihad* - meaning 'People Committed to the Propagation of the Prophet's Teachings and Jihad'. In the town of Maiduguri where the group was believed to have been formed, the residents call them 'Boko Haram', a combination of the Hausa word 'boko' meaning 'Western education' and the Arabic word 'Haram' which figuratively means 'sin' and literally means 'forbidden'. Boko Haram has therefore been commonly translated as 'Western education is sacrilege' or 'Western education is a sin'. Some scholars however believe that such is more of a transliteration of the two words, and that such a transliteration would be incapable of capturing what the original coiners of the words had in mind. What appears obvious however is that the group earned its name due to its strong opposition to anything Western, which it believes has a corrupting influence on Muslims (Chotia, 2012)

Ioannis Mantzikos (2010), a Greek researcher on Islamic movements, for instance suggested that what the users of the word 'Boko Haram' meant to convey is 'Western Civilisation is forbidden' rather than 'Western education' is forbidden' or a sacrilege. He argues that translating 'Boko' as 'Western education' in that context gives the false impression that the sect is opposed to formal education from the West when in actual fact what they are opposed to is Western civilization – which includes education but is not defined by it. He believes that by translating 'Boko Haram' as 'Western civilization is forbidden' it highlights the sect's belief in the supremacy of Islamic culture (Mantzikos, 2010:58). Mantzikos' position seems to be bolstered by the fact that before his death, the then leader of the sect, Muhammad Yusuf, was known not only to be opposed to the current education system but was also opposed to the country's democracy, and in fact anything Western - '"[i]f it runs contrary to the teachings of Allah" (Boyle, 2009).

Apart from 'Boko Haram' locals also call the group by other names such as 'Taliban' even though there is no evidence it has links with the Talibans of Afghanistan. In fact while some believe that the name 'Taliban' came about because the group was thought to have been inspired by the Talibans of Afghanistan, others say the locals used it more as a term of ridicule (Boyle, 2009). Boyle quoted one Isa Sanusi from the BBC Hausa Service as saying that the group has no specific name for itself, just many names attributed to it by local people.

The sect's teachings were initially Salafist. Salafis are said to have attributed the supposed decline of Islam after the early generations to the abandonment of pure Islamic teachings. They believe that Islamic revival can only come about by purging foreign influences from the doctrine and emulating the early generation of Muslims. Consequently the sect focused on the corruptive influences of Western civilisation and secularisation of the State. For instance the sect believes that women have become 'loose' because Westernisation and secularisation encouraged it.

They also believed that rather than make people enlightened and holy, Western education and its associated civilisation was churning out thieves, whores and gangsters because they are being taught the ways of the West, including its lewd language, dressing and godlessness (Boyle, 2009). It is generally believed that it is the mode of the sect's condemnation of the corruptive influences of Western form of education that made the locals call it 'Boko Haram' (ibid).

33

Adebayo Alonge (2012) has articulated the strategies through which the sect hopes to achieve its objective of ridding Islam of its alleged corruptive Western influences, including the secularisation of the State:

- Kill civilians who collaborate with state security agencies.
- Kill critics, especially Muslim clerics.
- Kill Christians or forcibly convert them.
- Bomb churches and prevent conventional worshipping by Christians.
- Bomb security infrastructure.
- Kill security personnel.
- Rob banks and churches.
- Organize jail breaks to free imprisoned members and other criminals.
- Threaten politicians who oppose their political patrons.
- Threaten Southerners and Christians to relocate from the North.
- Burn secular schools.

Alonge (2012) believe the sect wants to:

- Prevent the practice of Christianity in the North.
- Forcibly cause a relocation of the Christian and Southern populace from the North.
- Prevent criticism and uprising against them by the local Muslim populace.
- Achieve monopoly of the instruments of force and ultimately government in Northern Nigeria.
- Disrupt normal life, undermine the central government and build up resentment against Nigerian security forces with the aim of sparking off mass revolt by the local populace.
- Spark off sectarian violence nationwide by provoking Southerners to avenge the killings of their kin in the North.

What is obvious from the above is that the group is determined to use whatever means at its disposal, including terrorism, to achieve its goal. Since its avowed goal is to rid Islam of what it perceives as corruptive influences, it also means that the Muslims it identifies as propping up those corruptive influences or standing between it and its objectives are fair game.

Origin

Just as there are contestations over the name of the sect or the meaning of Boko Haram – the most popular of the names the locals of Maiduguri where it was believed to have been founded call it - there are also controversies over its origin. The popular belief is that it was founded around 2001 or 2002 by Mohammed Yusuf. Isioma Madike (2011) however disputes this, arguing that the sect was actually started in 1995 as *Sahaba* and was initially led by one Lawan Abubakar, who later left for further studies at the University of Medina in Saudi Arabia. Yusuf was said to have taken over the leadership after the departure of Abubakar and indoctrinated the sect with his own teachings, which he claimed were based on purity. According to this version, when Yusuf assumed leadership of the sect, he embarked on intensive and hugely successful membership recruitment. He was said to have over 500, 000 members before his demise. It was equally alleged that he taxed each member one Naira per day, meaning that he realized about N500,000 per day (Madike, 2011).

Whatever may be the truth about the origin of the sect, what is not in dispute is that Yusuf was responsible for raising its profile. He was in fact said to have established a religious complex that included a mosque and a school where many poor families from Nigeria and the neighbouring countries enrolled their children.

In 2004 the group extended the complex to Yusuf's home state of Yobe in the village of Kanamma near Niger State where it set up a base called Afghanistan (Aljazeera, 2009). Boko Haram followers, also called Yusuffiya, consist largely of hundreds of impoverished northern Islamic students and clerics as well as university students and professionals, many of whom are unemployed. It is suspected that some members of the Nigerian elite could be members of the sect (Johnson 2011).

The radicalisation of the group

There is fairly a consensus that until 2009 the group conducted its operations more or less peacefully and that its radicalisation followed a government clampdown in 2009 in which some 800 people, mostly members of the sect died (Adibe, 2011). Mohammed Yusuf was killed in that attack while in police custody. In what was apparently retaliation for the extra judicial killing of its leader, the group carried out its first terrorist attack in Borno in January 2010 at Dala Alemderi Ward in Maiduguri metropolis which resulted in the death of four people (Vanguard, online, December 10 2011). In January 2012, Abubakar Shekau, a former deputy to Yusuf, who was thought to have died in the government clampdown of 2009, appeared in a video posted on Youtube. According to Reuters' Joe Brock (2012) Shekau took control of the group after Yusuf's death in 2009.

Opinions differ on the reasons for the government clampdown in 2009. One opinion is that the government got wind that the group was arming itself and then struck. Another opinion traced this to a motorcycle incident. According to this version, some members of the sect were shot dead on June 11 2009 following a row with the police over the members' refusal to wear crash helmets in Maiduguri. Yusuf was said to have vowed to avenge the death of his members, which he allegedly did three days after the incident. On July 21 2009, nine members of the sect were arrested and paraded by the Borno State police command. The suspects were accused of being in possession of 74 empty locally-made bomb shells and explosive devices (Alonge, 2012). On July 26 2009, the sect members launched what was believed to be a reprisal attack on the police in Bauchi, the Bauchi State capital and spread their violence to other States in the North, - Borno, Bauchi, Yobe, Kano, Katsina and Sokoto (Brock, 2012).

Another version on why the sect got radicalised was that some politicians who were apparently using them as thugs became frightened when the sect became too powerful for them and therefore invited the government to deal with them. According to Adebayo Alonge (2012),

> ...before 2009, the group was under the influence of key politicians of Bornu. These men funded the sect and the flamboyant lifestyle of its leader- Mohammed Yusuf. Using his charismatic teachings and condemnation of the ills brought about by westernization e.g. immorality, poverty, drinking etc he was able to recruit thousands to his fold. Many graduates burned their certificates and University of Maiduguri students dropped out of school to join him. Workers left their jobs and Almajiris in their thousands sought protection from the hardships of their life from him.

Alonge (2012) claims that the support of the sect was crucial to the victory of Ali Modu Sheriff in the 2003 and 2007 general elections. As he puts it,

..in the violent politicking that has come to define Nigeria's own brand of democracy, his[Yusuf's] sect, given its numbers, was well funded to arm itself in pursuance of election victory for the ANPP. Is it then little wonder that in the 2011 elections, with the sect involved in a different mission under a new ideology of Abubakar Shekau, the erstwhile deputy to Mohammed Yusuf, the ANPP lost the Bornu South Senatorial District election to the PDP for the first time since the start of the new democratic era in 1999? The fact also that the group supported Ali Ndume against the then Bornu governor Ali Modu Sheriff points to the possibility of a splinter in the group. A part of the group may have wanted to punish the ANPP for withdrawing funding hence the new support for the PDP through Ndume who was a former ANPP stalwart and House of Representative member (2003-2011) under their platform.

The Government has since charged Ali Ndume, a Senator of the Federal Republic of Nigeria, to court for being one of the sponsors of Boko Haram – a charge he denies. As at the time of writing (August, 2012), the case is still in court.

References

Adibe, Jideofor (2012a): 'Boko Haram as a symptom of the crisis in Nigeria's nation-building project (paper presented at the Institute for Security Studies, Pretoria, South Africa, February 2, 2012)

Adibe, Jideofor (2012b): 'Boko Haram: One sect, conflicting narratives', *African Renaissance*, Volume 9 Number 1 2012, pp47-64

Adibe, Jideofor (2011) 'Beyond Boko Haram' *Daily Trust*, September 1, (back page)

Aljazeera 2009: 'Deadly Nigeria Clashes Spread: At least 60 people killed as police battle Islamist group in four northern states' in http://www.aljazeera.com/news/africa/2009/0 7/2009727134953755877.html (Retrieved January 30, 2012).

Alonge, Adebayo (2012) 'Solving the Boko Haram Menace', March 12.
http://adebayoalonge.wordpress.com/2012/03/11/solving-the-boko-haram-menace/
(Retrieved, June 13 2012)

Boyle, Joe 2009: 'Nigeria's 'Taliban' enigma'
http://news.bbc.co.uk/2/hi/africa/8172270.stm
(Accessed March 24, 2012)

Brock, Joe (2012) 'Nigeria sect leader defends killings in video' in
http://af.reuters.com/article/topNews/idAFJOE80B01D20120112, Jan 12 , Accessed January 30

Chothia, Farouk (2012), 'Who are Nigeria's Boko Haram Islamists' in BBC News Africa, January 11
http://www.bbc.co.uk/news/world-africa-13809501, (Accessed March 31 2012).

Johnson, Toni (2011) 'Boko Haram' (Council for Foreign Relations blog),

http://www.cfr.org/africa/boko-
haram/p25739, Dec 27(Accessed January 29,
2012)

Madike, Isioma (2011)'Boko Haram: Rise of
a deadly sect', in National Mirroe 19/06/2011
http://www.nationalmirroronline.net/sunday-
mirror/big_read/14548.html (Accessed March
24, 2012)

Mantzikos, Ioannis (2010): 'The absence of
state in Northern Nigeria: The case of Boko
Haram', *African Renaissance* Vol 7 No. 1 57-
62

Vanguard (2011): "Boko Haram: Has
Northern leaders found their voice?" Dec. 10,
2011
http://www.vanguardngr.com/2011/12/boko-
haram-has-northen-leaders-found-their-voice/
(Accessed January 30 2012).

CHAPTER 3

EXPLAINING THE BOKO HARAM PHENOMENON

How do we explain the emergence of a sect like Boko Haram and their ability to recruit members, apparently in droves, in the North-east part of the country? Like virtually everything about the sect, there have been several explanations and 'theories' on why they emerged and thrive. We examine some of these explanations:

The historical explanation

It is here argued that prior to colonialism the Bornu Empire ruled the territory where Boko Haram is currently active. It was an independent sultanate dominated by Kanuri Muslims and modelled after the Constitution of Medina. The Bornu sultanate came into being after the overthrow of the Kanem-Bornu Empire, which was ruled by the

Saifawa dynasty for over 2000 years. The Kanuri-dominated Bornu sultanate differed from the Sokoto Caliphate, which was established by the Hausa/Fulani in 1802 following Usman dan Fodio's military victory. In 1903, both the Bornu Sultanate and the Sokoto Caliphate came under the control of the British.

The Kanuris were said to be suspicious of the early Christian missionaries and feared that they used Western education as a tool for evangelisation. It is thought that the roots of religious fundamentalism were sown among the Kanuris and in the North-east in general during this period (Wikipedia, no date).

A major problem with this explanation is that it implies that terrorism or fundamentalism is inherent among the Kanuris because of its history. While this may be partly true, this explanation is inadequate because it fails to tell us why such fundamentalism is not widespread among the Kanuri and why similar fundamentalism periodically erupts among some non-Kanuri populations in the

North such as the periodic religious eruptions in Kaduna, Kano, Jos and other cities in the North. In fact one of the most infamous of such riots was the Maitatsine riots of the 1980s, which took place, not in the North east but in Kano, though some people have tried to trace an affinity between the sect and Boko Haram.

The failed state argument

Some people have suggested that Boko Haram is simply a symptom that the Nigerian State has failed, or at best, is failing. There is no consensus on the meaning of 'failed state' including how to 'operationalise' it (see William Easterly and Laura Freschi, 2010). The difficulty of defining it is compounded by the fact that it is sometimes used as a tool of political blackmail such that anyone can focus on where a state is perceived as not doing well – such as in the provision of security, welfare or improving the standard of living of its people - and then conclude, based on that, that the State in question has 'failed' or is 'failing'.

47

The closest to an extant taxonomy for measuring a failed state is the Failed State Index published since 2005 by Fund for Peace, an independent Washington DC-based non-profit research and educational institution. The Index, which is published in conjunction with the magazine *Foreign Policy*, uses the following to determine the extent to which a state has failed or is failing:

1. Loss of control of its territory, or of the monopoly on the legitimate use of physical force.
2. Erosion of legitimate authority to make collective decisions.
3. Inability to provide public services, and
4. Inability to interact with other states as a full member of the international community

Table 2: Nigeria's ranking in the Failed State Index

Year	Rank
2007	17
2008	19
2009	15
2010	14
2011	14
2012	14

Source: compiled from various tables of Failed State Index, 2007-2012.

Nigeria entered the league of the worst 20 cases in 2007 before Boko Haram unleashed its terrorist activities. The implication is that while Boko Haram was not responsible for Nigeria moving into the league of infamy of the worst 20 cases of failed or failing state, it contributed to the worsening of its ranking.

Since the Failed State Index appears to have become the central reference source in many development circles and among many civil society organisations in the annual binary delineation of failed and not failed states, it may perhaps be germane to make a few remarks about the Index, which is published alongside the so-called Postcards from Hell – a gallery of some of the world's most troubled states:

One, indices are notoriously difficult to construct and even harder to perfect amid competing methodologies and data sources. The Failed State Index uses several parameters, most of them subjectively determined– population pressures, the number of refugees in a country, how factionalised the elites of a country are, a state's capacity to provide public services, extent of uneven development and of course a state's ability to enforce its statutory monopoly of legitimate instruments of coercion in its domain.

Overall, the Index's headline indicators are weighted summaries from more than 100 sub-indicators. Like most indices of this nature, conclusions you reach will often depend on your initial assumptions on each parameter. It is really on the underlying assumptions that value judgments get loaded, triggering controversies in the process. For instance just by relying on a different set of assumptions, Noam Chomsky, the American linguist, historian and activist, in his famous book, *Failed States: The Abuse of Power and the Assault on Democracy* (2006) argues that the US itself was becoming a 'failed state' and therefore a danger to its people.

The obvious methodological weaknesses in the compilation of the Failed State Index for instance makes it unable to capture the important differences between state collapse, state failure and state fragility, leading to an unhelpful ossification of the three into the unhelpful binary of failed or not failed states (Adibe, 2012a).

Obviously because the Failed State Index – like most other indices - try to capture the variables on which it is measuring and ranking states in statistical forms, it comes out looking impressive. However as the American writer Darrel Huff tells us in his very influential book *How to Lie With Statistics* (1954), you can use figures, graphs and tables to hoodwink and blackmail or to make yourself appear cleverer than you really are. The Failed State Index – intentionally or unintentionally has been able to do just this for years - and getting away with it.

Two, it may not be out of place to interrogate the motive of the sponsors of the Failed State Index. If the aim is to provide early warning systems, then there are already several institutions and programmes devoted to studying potentially vulnerable spots such as the Crisis State Research Centre at the London School of Economics.

There is a suspicion among some development scholars that the Index may not be unlinked with a desire to rejuvenate the 'help industry' in the West. Obviously as the traditional areas of 'help' – fighting famine in the Horn of Africa, AIDS in Africa, landmines, child soldiers from Africa etc begin to lose their allure, the 'help industry' that creates lucrative jobs for consultants appears to have come under pressure to justify the need for its continued existence or why it should be given new money. Some critics have wondered whether the Failed State Index is one such creative way of ensuring that the 'help industry' continues to retain its significance because if states are designated as failing there will obviously be a need to do something to build their capacity so that they do not fail and overwhelm the West with refugees.

Remarkably in April 2010, a group calling itself the G7+ was formed. It was supposed to be a group of seven 'of the world's most fragile states'. The membership of the group is said to have grown to 17 and the countries in the group claimed they came together to "share experiences" and "lobby international actors to engage more effectively in fragile and conflict-affected countries and regions" (Adibe, 2012). Cynics obviously want to know at whose instance the group was formed.

Three, the Failed State Index reinforces the essentialist construction of Africa and the narratives and innuendos that go with it. Over

99 percent of the worst performing countries in the index are from Africa and other parts of the developing world.

Agreed, many of the countries in Africa and the developing world are underperforming economically. But a fundamental reason why they underperform is the condition of underdevelopment which has several economic and non-economic symptoms or manifestations such as inability to provide public services and factionalised elites which engage in anarchic struggle for power because state power is often the most effective means of material accumulation in these countries.

Several of the symptoms of this fundamental problem of underdevelopment are already captured in a pick-and- choose manner by other indices such as the United Nations Human Development Index, the Ease of Doing Business Index among countries, the Sustainable Governance Index etc.

The condition of being underdeveloped economies naturally means that Africa's rankings in these indices will be low, explaining why African and other developing countries are the worst performers in virtually all available global indices. It is like four different indices each ranking people according to how healthy they look, their physical strength, how briskly they work and how fast they can run. A man who is severely ill with malaria and has suffered loss of appetite as a result will be poorly captured by each of the four indices even though his only problem is that he is suffering from malaria. Being poorly captured by each of the four indices will lead into a self-fulfilling prophecy – the man is no good and there are 'facts and figures' to back it up.

Africa and other underdeveloped countries are ranked low in several global indices because these indices are abstracting the symptoms of the fundamental problem of underdevelopment and elevating them to a defining characteristic of Africans are. This is both essentialist and reductionist. There is nothing genetic, geographic or racial about the African condition – contrary to the impression these indices give.

Four, there is also an impression that these Indices are being mischievously used by some Western countries to promote nationalism and internal cohesion by subtly letting their citizens know that as much as things may be difficult for them, they are infinitely better off than people in several countries and they can easily draw attention to the relative ranking of their countries in these indices. This 'feel good' factor is however created at the expense of others who may then become unwitting victims of institutionalised discrimination. For many in the West, the indices and their higher rankings in them are a confirmation of their inherent superiority. Will you then blame employers who, after reading several of such indices refuse to employ people from certain parts of the world? Have statistics not shown those people are not good enough?

Five, a critique of the Failed State Index is not to deny that several countries in Africa, including Nigeria, face serious challenges. As we have argued in this monograph, we believe that Nigeria has a severe crisis in its nation-building process. We do not believe that as a country we can make much progress, no matter what our purported growth figures tell us, without first resolving the crisis we face in the construction of a viable nation-state.

Given the above weaknesses of the Failed State Index therefore, to see the Boko Haram challenge as a sign of State failure by pointing out that we have already made it to the league of infamy in the Index, will be unhelpful. What I believe is happening with Boko Haram, especially the fact that it is mainly localised around the North-east is that more of the sub-states in the country are becoming 'failed cities', where the elected governments compete for hegemony with militarised gangs, religious fanatics, kidnappers, drug barons and organised political thugs. We may therefore be heading

57

towards a variant of the Brazilian model where we may have a successful country (if we believe the official growth rate of the economy) but with many failed sub-states (known also as the peripheria). It should be noted that Brazil has the world's fifth largest surface area, the fifth biggest population and perhaps the fifth biggest economy but with failed cities, (Braathen 2011). Nigeria with a official per capita income of $2,700 and a GDP growth rate of seven percent cannot be called a failed state – despite the current security challenges (we are taking these highly suspect figures as given).

Human needs and poor governance theory

Human Needs theorists such as John Burton (1990) and Abraham Maslow (1943) would argue that one of the primary causes of protracted conflicts is people's drive to meet their unmet needs. Though Burton did not invent the theory, which asserts the existence of certain universal needs that must be satisfied if people are to prevent or resolve destructive conflicts, he gave it one of its most impassioned and uncompromising expressions. In *Deviance, Terrorism and War* Burton acknowledged his debt to Paul Sites, whose *Control: The Basis of Social Order* (1973) defined eight essential needs whose satisfaction was required in order to produce "normal" (i.e. non-deviant and non-violent) individual behaviour. According to Sites, these included the primary needs for consistency of response, stimulation, security, and recognition, and derivative needs for justice, meaning, rationality, and control. Sites, in turn, recognized the importance of Abraham Maslow's conception of human development as the sequential satisfaction of basic needs, which Maslow (1943) had grouped under five headings: physiological, safety, belongingness/love, esteem, and self-actualisation.

Burton made a distinction between disputes and conflicts. For him, while a dispute revolves conflicting, but negotiable interests, conflict develops around nonnegotiable issues of basic human needs deprivation. Settlement implies negotiated or arbitrated solutions, while resolution is concerned with satisfaction of basic human needs of all parties involved. He argued that "deterrence cannot deter" –meaning that coercive methods will be insufficient to modify behaviour when individuals or groups are impelled to act on the basis of imperative needs.

Those who have sought to explain the Boko Haram phenomenon within this framework point out that despite official per capita income of $2,700 and annual GDP growth of seven percent, the North – the main base of Boko Haram's activities - has one of the poorest populations in Nigeria. The economic disparities between the north and the rest of the country are stark. For instance in the north, 72 percent of people live in poverty compared to 27 percent in the south and 35 percent in the Niger Delta (Adibe, 2012b). Within the North itself the North-east, the base of Boko Haram's operations, has one of the largest concentrations of those Franz Fanon (2001) would call the 'Wretched of the

Earth', many of whom are either unemployed or underemployed.

Some analysts (see for instance Alonge, 2012) have also attributed the relative poverty of the North to 'bad governance' by the Governors of the states in the region, who are accused of embezzling or misappropriating the funds that should have been channelled to the development of their States.

We will argue that while there are some merits in both the human needs and poor governance arguments, this cannot comprehensively explain the audacity of the sect's actions or why a similar group has not emerged in other impoverished parts of the country. Besides, poor governance is not exclusive to the States in the North, and there is actually no evidence that the States in other parts of the country are better governed.

Relative Deprivation thesis

Ted Gurr (1970), one of the world's leading authorities on political conflicts and instability, in his highly influential book, *Why Men Rebel* (1970) emphasized the importance of socio-psychological factors (relative deprivation) as root sources of political violence based on perceived discrepancies between one's value expectations and one's value capabilities. This is also known as action-reaction theory. According to Gurr (1970:25), people "are quick to aspire beyond their social means and quick to anger when those means prove inadequate, but slow to accept their limitations". In essence, if there is a discrepancy between what people think they are entitled to and what they can achieve, such a discrepancy, he argues, holds the potential for political violence. The irony, according to Gurr, is that if what people think they can achieve and what they end up receiving differ, they often justify such by blaming it on others. In the book Gurr gives a long review of psychological research on aggression and concludes that frustration-aggression is the "primary source of the human capacity for violence" (p.36). For Gurr Relative deprivation can occur in one or more of three ways:

- "Decremental deprivation" - where value expectations remain constant while capabilities fall.
- "Aspirational Deprivation" - where value expectations rise while capabilities remain the same.
- "Progressive deprivation" – where value expectations grow and capabilities also grow but capabilities either don't keep up with the growth in value expectations or start to fall:

There are several explanations of the Boko Haram phenomenon, which allude to an endemic 'crisis of relative deprivation' in the North, which are then externalised as violence. Again while this may be partly true, we will argue that this thesis cannot comprehensively explain the Boko Haram phenomenon or why similar sects have not emerged in several other parts of the country where most of the citizens suffer from one form of relative deprivation or the other.

The Frustration-Aggression Hypothesis

The frustration-aggression hypothesis otherwise known as frustration-aggression displacement theory (see for instance Dollard et al, 1939) argues that frustration causes aggression, but when the source of the frustration cannot be challenged, the aggression gets displaced onto an innocent target.

There are a number of explanations of the reasons for the emergence of the Boko Haram phenomenon that would appear to fit into this theory. For instance the CBN Governor Sanusi Lamido Sanusi was quoted by ThisDay of January 28 2012 as blaming the rise of Boko Haram partly on the principle of derivation. According to him a "revenue sharing formula that gave 13 percent derivation to the oil-producing states was introduced after the military relinquished power in 1999 among a series of measures aimed at redressing historic grievances among those living closest to the oil and quelling a conflict that was

64

jeopardising output." He was further quoted as saying: "There is clearly a direct link between the very uneven nature of distribution of resources and the rising level of violence" (ibid).

While this may be partly true - it cannot comprehensively explain why the Boko Haram type of violence is not generalised in the North or why several states in the South which do not benefit from the 13% derivation have also not taken to militancy.

Senator Uche Chukwumerije has also argued that Boko Haram is all about the presidential election in 2015 (see The Nation, online September 29 2011). In his view, President Goodluck Jonathan's emergence as president was facilitated by the activities of the Niger Delta militants. He equally believes the militancy of the Oodua Peoples' Congress (OPC) in the Yoruba agitation to win the Presidency facilitated the emergence of Obasanjo, a Yoruba, as a civilian President in 1999. For Senator Chukwumerije who represents Aba North in Nigeria's Senate, Boko Haram, is merely trying to follow in the

65

footsteps of MEND and OPC. He called on the Igbo militia MASSOB , to "devise a means of constructive engagement with the youth" so that they "should stop behaving like somebody stung by a bee and flees at a mere hum of a house fly" (Ibid).

Apart from what would appear to be a tacit encouragement of violence in the name of laying an overwhelming claim to what a group believes to be its entitlement to rule, it is not very correct to argue that violence or militancy was what won the Yoruba and the Niger Delta power. I have elsewhere (Adibe, 2012c) argued that in a society like Nigeria, the way the narrative of a struggle is framed will play a significant role in the base of support it attracts and that no ethnic group or region can win the presidency of the country without substantial support from other parts of the country. For instance NADECO which played a crucial role in the struggle for the re-validation of Abiola's mandate after an election he won in June 1993 was annulled by the Babangida regime, framed the narrative of its struggle in altruistic terms – namely as a struggle for democracy which helped to increase the base of its support. For the Niger Delta, its struggle was largely framed as a campaign against environmental degradation caused by oil exploration in the area – and this helped the area to attract international attention and sympathy. While it is true that MEND's militancy helped to attract attention to its cause, it is doubtful if its struggle would have succeeded in making someone from Niger Delta to become the President without the death of Yaradua and the support of other Nigerians that Jonathan should succeed him. Largely because of this, it is doubtful if Boko Haram, which formally says it wants to establish an Islamic state and MASSOB which wants the State of Biafra would be able to mobilize sufficient support from other Nigerians to achieve their avowed objectives.

A variant of the frustration-aggression response popular with some explanations of the Boko Haram phenomenon is that after the reintroduction of Sharia law in the 12 Northern states, there was a widespread disillusionment at the way it was implemented, and members of the sect simply tapped into that frustration. As Jean Herskovits, an expert on Nigerian politics was quoted as saying about it: "You punish somebody for stealing a goat or less--but a governor steals billions of *naira*, and gets off scot-free," (quoted in Johnson, 2011).

There is also a belief that in Nigeria's mode of sharing privileges, the Igbo controls the commercial economy, the Yoruba the corporate economy and the North, political power. The loss of power to the south is therefore seen as loss of the North's lever in maintaining the power balance, which creates frustrations that Boko Haram tapped into, especially following the fall-outs from the ruling party's bickering over zoning and power sharing arrangements and President Jonathan's decision to contest the April 2011 elections.

Conspiracy theories

There are several conspiracy theories about Boko Haram. One, which is popular among commentators from the Southern part of the country, is that the sect is sponsored by key Northern politicians to make the country 'ungovernable' for President Goodluck Jonathan, a Southerner from the minority Ijaw ethnic group. According to this view, the North, essentially the 'core North', believes it is their birth right to govern the country, and because a Christian Southerner is in charge, they decided to sponsor Boko Haram as an instrument for destabilising the Jonathan presidency.

One of the weaknesses of this 'theory' is that much of the mayhem carried out by the sect has been in the North and against Northern Muslims. It is in fact difficult to see the nexus between destabilising governance in some Northern states, essentially in the North-east, and making the country 'ungovernable' for the Jonathan administration.

Another conspiracy theory is that Boko Haram is actually being sponsored by the Jonathan administration to make Islam look bad or give the impression that the North was out to pull it down as a way of mobilising the support of his 'Southern brethren' behind his

69

administration. Those who believe in this 'theory', essentially people from the North, point out that during the Abacha days, the government deliberately bombed some places and then blamed it on NADECO and that the Jonathan administration is doing the same.

One of the weaknesses of this theory however is that nothing in the confessions of some of the arrested Boko Haram members support this 'theory'. Again nothing in the Youtube or press releases by Shekau, thought to be the leader of the group, supports this.

Another conspiracy theory is that Boko Haram is actually a 'secret society'. I once received an email by one who claimed to be a former member of the sect swearing that the sect is made up of Christians, "including a former President from the South", Muslims and even adherents of traditional religion. It claimed that the aim of the sect is to "destroy the North before 2015", that is before the next election cycle, when the North is expected to make a strong bid for the presidency of the country. In another breath the email also claimed that the sect was actually paid to destroy Nigeria "using the name of Islam". The sender of the email concluded with: "May Allah expose us the more, Ameen". It is not very difficult to see the subtext in this 'theory', and I don't believe 'theories' like this are worth much consideration even though as conspiracy theories go, there are always people ever ready to believe anything.

External Linkages

One of the questions often asked these days is whether Boko Haram now has linkages with Al Quaeda, especially given the increasing sophistication of its methods and the audacity of its atrocities? The government thinks so. In fact in June 2009 the Nigerian State Security Service claimed that members of Boko Haram were being trained in Afghanistan and Algeria by members of al-Qaeda. For instance a day after the bombing of the UN building in Abuja on August 26 2011, President Jonathan was said to have stood in front of the smouldering rubble and declared: "Boko Haram is a local group linked up with terrorist activities and as a government we are

71

working on it and we will bring it under control" (cited in Bartolotta, 2011). Golwa and Alozieuwa (2012:77) in fact argue that while Boko Haram initially appeared as a local sect with little or no outside connection,

"...later developments indicate that the sect might have, from the onset, been part of the al Qaeda and the Salafi Jihad Movement affiliates that were encouraged to be established abroad as a result of the successful destruction of Al Qaeda's infrastructure in Afghanistan in late 2001 through the United States-led Operation Enduring Freedom.

For Golwa and Alozieuwa, following the loss of its Afghan sanctuary, Al Qaeda continued to encourage and promote the global Salafi Jihad movement. They gave example of how, an apparently indigene versus settler conflagration in Jos (North Central Nigeria) but which manifested as a dispute between Muslims and Christians prompted the Al Qaeda in the Islamic Maghreb (AQIM) to volunteer to train the Nigerian Moslems involved in the conflict in weapon handling. AQIM was also said to have promised to give Muslims involved in the conflict whatever they needed – men, arms and ammunition – to enable them defend themselves.

Golwa and Alozieuwa (2012) also draw several similarities in the operational methods of Boko Haram with those of Al Qaeda and other international terrorist organizations and concluded that Boko Haram not only has affiliation with groups like Al Shabaab and AQIM but probably did so at a very early stage of the sect's formation.

The idea that Boko Haram could be linked to other international terrorist groups especially the Al Qaeda in the Islamic Maghreb (AQIM) received a boost when the United States in June 2012 designated three leaders of Boko Haram – Abubakar Shekau, widely believed to lead Boko Haram's main Islamist cell, Abubakar Adam Kambar and Khalid al-Barnawi- as terrorists Vanguard (2012a). Surprisingly the Nigerian government, which had given the impression that Boko Haram had links with other terrorist organisations opposed plans by the US to formally declare Boko Haram as a terrorist group. Nigeria's Ambassador to the United States Proessor Ade Adefuye claimed that the country's position was informed by fears that such "classification will subject innocent Nigerian travellers to undue embarrassment and humiliation from America's immigration authorities" (Vanguard 2012b). He was further quoted as saying:

> …some members of the Republican Party in the U.S. Congress have been mounting pressure on the Obama administration to classify Boko Haram as a Foreign Terrorist Organisation, but Nigeria is opposed to it because it will elevate the status of Boko Haram and embolden them. The classification could pave way for the U.S. to use its unmanned drones to attack the leadership of the group. (Ibid)

The Ambassador reportedly said that experience from Afghanistan and Pakistan showed that such unmanned drones could lead to the destruction of villages and people who are not directly involved in the activities of Boko Haram.

While the Ambassador's explanation makes sense – given the likelihood that any attack on villages that leads to heavy casualties could easily be politicized - it does not conclusively address the question of whether Boko Haram is indeed working in cahoots with other international terrorist organizations.

Despite the increasing suspicion that Boko Haram could be affiliated to other international terrorist organisations largely because of the increasing audacity and sophistication of its methods, not everyone believes that. The former US ambassador to Nigeria John Campbell (quoted in Bartolotta, 2011) and Mantizikos (2010), an expert on Islamic movements, argue that there are no hard evidence of such a linkage - though in another article (see Baken and Mantzikos, 2012), Mantizikos seems to have changed his position on this.

It can be argued that the Nigerian government has a vested interest in presenting Boko Haram as having such a linkage. One, it will make it easier to attract international sympathy and technical assistance from European countries and USA which since September 11 have been especially sensitive about the name Al Qaeda and can get quite paranoid about any group rumoured to be linked to it. Two, linking Boko Haram to Al-Qaeda will be face-saving, making it easier for the government to rationalise its inability to contain the group and its activities – after all, if the USA and the European countries have not been able to defeat Al Quaeda , why will anyone see it as a sign of weakness that an African government has not been able to defeat an organisation it sponsors? Three, by linking Boko Haram to Al Qaeda, the government may hope to use innuendos and name-dropping of US involvement to frighten the sect and help to pressure it to the negotiating table.

However there are also concerns that if Boko Haram does not already have such an external linkage, it will also be in its interest that it is being portrayed as an organisation working in cahoots with the dreaded Al Qaeda. Such a portraiture will not only increase the awe with which it is held but may also even help it to attract the attention and sympathy of Al Qaeda and similar terrorist organisations. The paradox here is that if the USA gets openly involved in fighting Boko Haram, it will galvanize the support of anti- USA forces globally and even domestically behind the sect. It could also fire off a wave of nationalism that may end up winning the sect sympathisers even from Nigerians stoutly opposed to the sect's activities. It may in fact be argued that the sect's attack on the UN was not only aimed at raising its profile but also to use any internationalisation of the fight against it for recruitment purposes. A similar thing could be said about its attacks on churches. Perhaps it hopes that such attacks could lead to a sectarian war which will be a veritable source of membership recruitment for the sect.

Linking Boko Haram to international terrorist organisations is therefore like the Devil's alternative for the government. It needs such a linkage to attract international sympathy and assistance and blunt domestic criticisms that it is weak on security. On the other hand talks of such linkages, if Boko Haram does not already have one, increases the likelihood that it will get the attention and sympathy of Al Qaeda and similar international terrorist groups, especially with the expectation that the US and Europe would get involved. Again if Boko Haram actually has an external linkage, the government will lack the capacity to fight it on its own, meaning an inevitable involvement of the US and other European countries, which will facilitate membership recruitment for Boko Haram.

References

Adibe, (2012a) 'Failed State Index as a tool of Imperialism', *Daily Trust*, July 5 (back page).

Adibe, Jideofor (2012b): 'Boko Haram: One sect, conflicting narratives', *African Renaissance*, Volume. 9 Number 1 2012, pp47-64

Adibe, Jideofor (2012c) , 'Ciroma Group's Big Mistake', *Daily Trust*, January 26, (back page).

Alonge, Adebayo (2012): 'Solving the Boko Haram Menace' (March 12). http://adebayoalonge.wordpress.com/2012/03 /11/solving-the-boko-haram-menace/ (Accessed, June 13 2012)

Baken, Dennis N and I. Mantzikos (2012): 'The Cyber Terrorism Shadow Networks in Africa: AQIM and Boko Haram (2012), *African Renaissance* Volume 9 No. 1 pp27-45.

Bartolotta , Christopher (2011) 'Terrorism in Nigeria: The rise of Boko Haram', *The Whitehead Journal of Diplomacy and International Relations,* Sept 23

(http://blogs.shu.edu/diplomacy/2011/09/terro rism-in-nigeria-the-rise-of-boko-haram/ (Accessed January 30 2012)

Braathen, Einar (2011) in the blog 'Brazil: Successful Country, Failed Cities?' http://blog.nibrinternational.no/#post30 (January 24 2011, Accessed January 30)

Burton, John (1990) *Conflict Resolution and Prevention* (New York: St. Martin's Press,)

Burton, John (1979): *Deviance, Terrorism and War: The Process of Solving Unsolved Social and Political Problems* (Basingstoke, Palgrave Macmillan)

Chomsky, Noam (2006): *Failed States: The Abuse of Power and the Assault on Democracy* (London, Metropolitan Books)

Dollard, Miller et al. (1939). *Frustration and aggression,* (New Haven, Yale University Press)

Fanon, Frantz (2001 edition), *Wretched of the Earth* (London, Penguin Classics)

Freschi, Laura and Easterly William (2010): 'Top Five Reasons why 'failed State' is a failed concept' http://aidwatchers.com/2010/01/top-5-reasons-why-%E2%80%9Cfailed-state%E2%80%9D-is-a-failed-concept/.,January 13; (Accessed, January 30).

Golwa, J. P. and Simeon H.O. Alozieuwa (2012): 'Perspectives on Nigeria's Security Challenges: The Niger Delta Militancy and Boko Haram Insurgency Compared', African Renaissance Volume 9 No. 1, pp65-90

Gurr, Ted R. (1970): Why *Men Rebel,* (Princeton, Princeton University Press)

Huff, Daniel (1954): *How to Lie With Statistics* http://www.scribd.com/doc/56279818/How-to-Lie-With-Statistics-Daniel-Huff-1954 (Accessed August 12, 2012)

Johnson, Toni (2011) 'Boko Haram' (Council for Foreign Relations blog), http://www.cfr.org/africa/boko-haram/p25739, Dec. 27 (Accessed January 29, 2012)

Mantzikos, Ioannis (2010): 'The absence of state in Northern Nigeria: The case of Boko Haram', *African Renaissance* Vol. 7 No. 1 57-62

Maslow, Abraham H (1943): *A Theory of Human Motivation*, *Psychological Review* 50(4): 370-96

Sites, Paul (1973) Control: *The Basis of Social Order* (New York, Dunellen Pub Co.)

The Nation, online September 29 2011 Chukwumerije on Boko Haram

ThisDay (2012): 'Sanusi Links Boko Haram to Derivation', January 28 http://www.thisdaylive.com/articles/sanusi-links-boko-haram-to-derivation/108039/ (accessed July 20, 2012)

Vanguard (2012a) :'US declares Abubakar Shekau, 2 others as terrorists', June 12 http://www.vanguardngr.com/2012/06/us-declares-abubakar-shekau-2-others-terrorists/ (Accessed July 28, 2012)
.

Vanguard (2012b,): 'Why FG resists terrorist label for Boko Haram – Ambassador', August 15 http://www.vanguardngr.com/2012/08/why-fg-resists-terrorist-label-for-boko-haram-ambassador/ (Accessed August 10, 2012)

Wikipedia (no date): 'Boko Haram' http://en.wikipedia.org/wiki/Boko_Haram (Accessed July 20, 2012)

CHAPTER 4

CRISIS IN NIGERIA'S NATION-BUILDING

We will argue that a more comprehensive explanation of the Boko Haram phenomenon is the crisis in our nation-building project. Our position is that all the efforts at fashioning a nation-state from the colonially inherited state nation seem to have stalled. Let's do a brief evaluation of those efforts:

Adoption of a federal constitution

Virtually everyone agrees that Nigeria's federalism is nothing but unitarism in a federal clothing, hence the clamour today for the enthronement of 'true federalism', 'resource control' the resolution of the 'national question' or the convening of a 'sovereign national conference'. The latter is often a euphemism for a convening of a meeting of the federating units to decide if they still want to live together in one country, and if so, under what structural arrangements. We have also several groups making various agitations – ranging from those clamouring for greater autonomy within the Nigerian federation (as advocates of 'resource control' seem to be doing) to the various ethnic militia that aggressively protect or espouse sectional interests such as the OPC for the South-West, MASSOB for South-east, Arewa People's Congress for the Hausa/Fulani and MEND for the South-South.

One area where the crisis in our federalism manifests most is not only in the system of sharing revenues between the Federal, State and Local Governments but also on the principles to be used in sharing the money among the different tiers of government. Generally the Southern part of the country complains that the North has far more States and more local governments than the South and since these are units that share the revenue from the Federation Account, that the system gives unfair advantage to the North.

86

All the States and Local Governments in the country since 1967 were created by the various military regimes. All of these military rulers – with the exception of the Obasanjo regime - were led by officers of Northern origin. Even within the South, the South- east complains that it has the fewest number of states among all the geopolitical zones in the country and therefore disadvantaged in the quantum of revenue that flows to the region from the Federation Account. Most of the States in the South complain that they have less number of Local Governments than their counterparts in the North and therefore disadvantaged in the system of revenue allocation.

The North too has its grouse against the current structure of the country. In March 2012 for instance the Northern Governors' Forum took umbrage at the 13 percent derivation principle used in sharing revenue among the States and Local Governments from the Federation Account, arguing that the system disadvantages the North (Adibe, 2012). Governor Babangida Aliyu, who is

87

Chairman of the Northern Governors Forum, was particularly livid that revenues from offshore explorations are treated as being derived from the Niger Delta, when in his opinion, they shouldn't.

The Governor of the Central Bank, Lamido Sanusi Lamido, who is from the North, had set the stage by attributing the rise of Boko Haram to the 13 percent derivation , which the oil-bearing States of the Niger Delta receive from the Federation Account (ThisDay, January 28 2012). He was quoted as saying: "There is clearly a direct link between the very uneven nature of distribution of resources and the rising level of violence." It is however germane to note that derivation - a percentage of the revenues, which states retain from taxes on oil and other natural resources produced in their state – is only one of about five main criteria used in sharing revenue from the Federation Account. Historically, the bulk of the allocation (about 70 per cent) has been on the basis of 'equality of states' and 'population'.

Even within the geopolitical zones, there are several contradictions: in the North, there is the apparent contradiction between the Muslims and the Christians; in the South South, the Movement for the Survival of Ogoni People recently declared its autonomy. The President of MOSOP Dr Goodluck Diiigbo explained that what MOSOP declared was political autonomy for Ogoni people in Nigeria. He was quoted as saying: "It is internal autonomy, which means self-government within Nigeria in accordance with the United Nations declaration on rights of indigenous peoples" (Vanguard, 2012). In a related development in the same south-south geopolitical zone, members of the Bayelsa State House of Assembly on August 8 2012 voted overwhelmingly in support of a Bill for the creation of a state flag and Coat of Arms, as well as the adoption of an Ijaw anthem for the people (Guardian, 2012). The Bill, which entered its second reading, was sponsored by the Leader of the House, Peter Akpe, who was quoted as saying:

> As Bayelsans, we have come of age to be proud
> of where we come from as the only homogenous
> Ijaw state. The Bill, when passed into law, will
> be awakening our pride and honour reflected by
> the flag with a colour that is peculiar to our
> identity as a people (ibid).

There have been speculations about the
import of the move by the Bayelsa State
House of Assembly and whether it was the
beginning of a secessionist move. What is
clear from the above is that the adoption of
federalism - or more correctly the system of
federalism being practised in the country has
not been able to give the country the desired
unity in diversity. On the contrary the way the
federalism is practised appears to have also
become part of the problem.

Reflection of Federal Character

As discussed in Chapter 1, the federal
character provision in Nigeria's constitution
is meant to give every unit of the federation
the proverbial 'sense of belonging' and
ensure that no unit is marginalized. In
practice, this constitutional provision has

come under attack from two fronts – from those who believe it is not being respected enough and from those who argue that it privileges mediocrity over merit. Often the tendency has been for the various Presidents the country has had to skew the award of capital projects and strategic cabinet positions to people from his ethnic group or geopolitical zone. For instance the Punch of July 22 2012 reported that of contracts worth some N927 billion Naira awarded by President Jonathan in the first ten months after he was elected President in the April 2011 presidential elections, the Niger Delta where he comes from grabbed N246bn – or more than a quarter of all the contracts awarded during the period. In fact the trend has been for whichever ethnic group or geopolitical zone that produced the President to develop a certain sense of triumphalism, a certain swagger that this is their time and they should be the ones calling the shots in the sharing of the proverbial national cake.

One of the consequences of the above is that other ethnic groups/geopolitical zones tend to develop envy and loathing for the ethnic group/geopolitical zone that produced the President, which often manifests in finding fault with whatever the President or the ethnic/geopolitical zone in power does.

NYSC

As indicated in Chapter 1, the National Youth Service Corp scheme was set up in 1973 to further the goal of building unity in diversity by ensuring that graduates from universities and other institutions of higher learning who are under the age of thirty serve their nation for one year in states other than their own. For many years, the NYSC scheme was very useful in overcoming certain stereotypes by people who believed that the sun rose and set only in their own part of the country.

Though there had been discussions even before the Boko Haram challenge on whether the NYSC scheme was still delivering on its original mandate, the security challenge in many parts of the country – Boko Haram in the North, kidnapping in the south-east and communal/ethno-religious crises in many parts of the country have led to increasing number of participants in the scheme influencing where they want to serve. The killing of nine youth corps members in Bauchi and Kaduna states during the post-election violence that erupted in parts of the country after the April 2011 presidential elections coupled with the increasing audacity of the attacks by groups suspected to be Boko Haram members, have meant that many youth corps members from the south no longer want to serve in the North. In the same vein, there is a feeling that the fear of reprisal attacks in the South against Northerners for attacks by groups suspected to be Boko Haram members on churches and people from the south have made many Northern Youth corps members to choose to serve in the safety of their own region. What this implies is that the NYSC scheme, one of the very important nation-building projects, has also become engulfed in a crisis of relevance.

Creation of States

One of the key objectives of creating states in Nigeria – as discussed in Chapter 1 – was to bring government nearer to the people and by so doing not only promote development but also allow Nigerians to maintain their local peculiarities in the process.

In the 1950s, the agitation for state creation was predicated more on fears of domination by ethnic minorities. Today, despite the movement from 12 states in 1967 to the present 36 states since 1996, the agitation for the creation of more states has continued unabated. The irony is that despite the balkanisation of the States, State creation does not seem to either have effectively promoted unity in diversity or succeeded in allaying the fears of ethnic or cultural domination. On the contrary, each exercise has created new ethnic and cultural minorities, triggering in turn a fresh agitation for new states. Interestingly, no state creation exercise had been preceded by a referendum to determine the true feelings of the people to be affected. More often than not, new states are rewards to influential politicians with right connections, who champion the state creation exercise.

The cost of running the States is also not cheap: For instance each state has to maintain a Governor and his Deputy, commissioners, state legislators, a coterie of advisers, hangers-on, a new civil service etc. At the federal level, each state created will also add to the already bloated size of the federal government because of the constitutional provision that makes states the basic units used in determining whether the government is 'reflecting the federal character' in its appointments, composition of the federal public service and dispensation of privileges or not. This means that with each new state, the number of ministers, special advisers will necessarily be increased to ensure balanced representation of the number of states in appointments. Similarly each new state will have three senators and a certain number of Members of the House of Representatives. And we know it is not cheap to maintain the legislators!

One of the key issues in the politics of State creation is whether our historical experience shows that 'government being nearer to the people' (as advocates of state creation often believe) necessarily leads to the people 'feeling the effects of governance' in terms of the provision of infrastructure, jobs and physical and human security?

What seems to have happened is that State Creation has become become part of the problems of the country rather than a solution to certain problems. For instance because they are units for sharing revenues from the Federation Account the demand for more states from the various geopolitical zones appears to have become an issue of maintaining regional/ethnic pride and balance of power/privileges. For this, it seems to have worsened the anarchical character of Nigerian politics. For instance to be elected President of this country, there is a constitutional provision that a candidate must have no less than 25 percent of the votes cast at the election in each of at least two-thirds of all the states in the federation. This provision gives the number of states in each geopolitical zone a special political salience. Rival geopolitical or ethnic groups such as

North v South or *Yorubas v Igbos* routinely overheat the polity with their politics of state creation to ensure that they either maintain their current power balance or get more states in its zone to redress a perceived imbalance (Adibe, 2010)

Zoning

Zoning was one of the contrivances aimed at turning Nigeria from a state-nation into a nation-state by giving each unit of the country the proverbial sense of belonging and assuring them that they have an equal chance with every other area of the country to produce the key political officers of the country. However few issues have generated as much political acrimony as the PDP's zoning arrangement did in late 2010.

The North claimed that under the PDP's zoning and power rotation arrangements, the presidency of the country should return to the North after Olusegun Obasanjo, a Yoruba from the south- west has had two terms of four years each. It is generally believed that Obasanjo tried his best to amend the

97

constitution to 'elongate' his tenure but his moves were stoutly resisted by Nigerians. Obasanjo eventually anointed Umaru Yaradua as a successor. His critics however accuse him of deliberately foisting a sick man on the nation to further a certain political agenda.

When Umaru Yaradua died on 5 May 2010, many people from the North felt that Goodluck Jonathan, the Vice President under Yaradua, and an Ijaw from the South South, who succeeded Yaradua, should only serve out the four-year tenure of the late President but should not contest the 2011 presidential election as it was the turn of the North to produce the President. Many people from the south felt that Jonathan should contest, arguing that the North had dominated the country's politics for a long time. Suddenly a zoning arrangement that was introduced to give every part of the country a sense of belonging - as the politicians would say - became one of the most divisive issues in the country. It can be argued that Nigeria is yet to recover from the effects of that bitter acrimony over zoning and power rotation.

What appears obvious is that virtually every part of country claims it is 'marginalised', with some groups calling for the convocation of a Sovereign National Conference (a euphemism for a meeting to discuss whether Nigerians still want to continue to live together as one country or not). In fact all the past efforts and projects at building unity in diversity seem to be unravelling.

Clearly something nasty seems to have happened to the effort to create Nigerians to populate the geographical expression called Nigeria. It would seem that the crisis in our nation-building feeds into the crisis of underdevelopment to create an existentialist crisis for many Nigerians. For many young people, a way of resolving the consequent sense of alienation appears to be to retreat from the Nigeria project and construct meanings in chosen primordial identities - often with the Nigerian state as the enemy.

In Nigeria, there is a heavy burden of institutionalised sectional memories of hurt, injustice, distrust and even a disguised longing for vengeance. This means therefore that any strategy to confront the security challenge in the country is bound to evoke these ugly memories in some sections of the population. Largely because of the crisis in our nation-building and the consequent de-Nigerianisation which it triggered, no individual or political authority enjoys universal legitimacy across the main fault lines. Nigeria is therefore a country in which Nigerians seem to be stampeding out of the Nigeria project, raising the risk of having Nigeria without Nigerians.

We see Boko Haram as a manifestation of this crisis in our nation-building, where people exit the Nigeria project and try to negotiate meanings for their existence in a primordial identity with the state as an enemy. In other words, while the bombings and other unsavoury acts that are linked to the sect are very condemnable, it is germane to underline that Boko Haram is only one of

100

several groups in the country that purvey terror and death and regards the state and its institutions as enemies. This is not an apology for their actions, but there is an increasing tendency to discuss the spate of insecurity in the country as if it all began and ended with Boko Haram – or as if without Boko Haram Nigeria would be a tranquil place to live in. As I wrote elsewhere:

> The truth is that there is everywhere in the country a pervasive sense of what the German - American political theorist Hannah Arendt called the 'banality of evil'. Her explanation of this thesis is that the great evils in history are not executed by fanatics or sociopaths but rather by ordinary people who accepted the premises of their actions and therefore participated in them on the grounds that those heinous actions were normal. This is the so-called notion of 'normalising the unthinkable' or the routinisation of evil. And this truly reflects the federal character – violent armed robberies across the entire country, kidnapping especially in the South-east, turf war by militarised cults and gangs in Bayelsa State and senseless intra and inter communal 'warfare' across several parts of the country (Adibe, 2011)

101

With the Boko Haram attacks and many non-Northerners in the North fleeing back to their ethnic homelands, the de-Nigerianisation process is furthered. Similarly, with many Northerners fleeing the south for fear of reprisal attacks, a dagger is further thrust into the heart of the Nigeria project.

There is a suspicion that the number of Nigerians being alienated from the Nigeria project and therefore regarding the state as a legitimate target is increasing by leaps and bounds. If this trend continues, there is a big risk of having Nigeria without Nigerians as everyone seems to carry out an attack on the Nigerian state using whatever means at the person's disposal – those entrusted with the nation's common patrimony steal it blind, law enforcement officers turn the other way if you offer them a little inducement, organised labour, including university lecturers go on prolonged strikes on a whim, students resort to cultism and exam malpractices and workers drag their feet, refuse to put in their best and engage in moonlighting. Everyone seems to have one form of grouse or the other against the Nigerian state and its institutions.

References

Adibe, Jideofor (2012): 'The North, Revenue Allocation and the Games they Play' *Daily Trust*

Adibe, Jideofor (2011) 'Boko Haram as a symptom of the crisis in Nigeria's nation-building project'(paper presented to the Institute for Security Studies, Pretoria, South Africa, Feb. 2, 2012)

Adibe, Jideofor (2010) 'David Mark and the Agitation for More States' http://www.hollerafrica.com/showArticle.php?artId=412&catId=1&page=1(Accessed Aug 10, 2012)

ThisDay (2012): 'Sanusi Links Boko Haram to Derivation', January 28 http://www.thisdaylive.com/articles/sanusi-links-boko-haram-to-derivation/108039/ (accessed July 20, 2012)

Vanguard 2012 "We only declared political autonomy for Ogoni – MOSOP" (August 7), http://www.vanguardngr.com/2012/08/we-only-declared-political-autonomy-for-ogoni-mosop/ (Accessed August 12 2012)

Guardian (2012) 'Assembly plans Bayelsa State anthem, others', August 9. http://www.ngrguardiannews.com/index.php?option=com_content&view=article&id=9499 1:assembly-plans-bayelsa-state-anthem-others&catid=1:national&Itemid=559 (Accessed August 12 20120

Punch (2012): 'Jonathan awards N927bn contracts in 10 months, Niger Delta grabs N246bn', July 22 http://www.punchng.com/news/jonathan-awards-n927bn-contracts-in-10-months-%E2%80%A2niger-delta-grabs-n246bn/ (Accessed, August 11 2012)

CHAPTER 5

CONCLUSION AND
RECOMMENDATIONS

We have examined various aspects of the Boko Haram sect – the meaning of its name, its history, reasons for the sect's radicalisation, various theoretical expla-nations for its emergence, including whether it has linkages with other external terrorist groups such as Al Qaeda in the Maghreb (AQIM) and the Al Shabaab in Somalia. We argued that the common explanatory schemas, including the conspiracy theories that are often bandied around by some people, are inadequate to comprehensively explain the Boko Haram phenomenon. We contended that a more comprehensive explanation is to see the sect as one of the symptoms of the crisis in the country's nation-building.

What also emerged from our discussion is that in virtually every aspect of the sect, there are several, often conflicting narratives. This, in our opinion, is evidence that much of what is known about the sect remains at the realm of speculation and highlights an urgent need for a rigorous empirical research on the sect to fill the lacuna.

Beyond the Sovereign National Conference

There appears to be a consensus that something is implicitly wrong with the way that the country is configured and that there is a need by the constituent units to re-negotiate the basis of their togetherness. This belief has often found powerful echo in the calls for the convocation of a Sovereign National Conference (SNC) since the 1990s. Among its most famous advocates were the likes of the late Anthony Enahoro and Wole Soyinka (Kawu, 2012). But is SNC really a credible vehicle for resolving some of the contentious issues which had dominated national discourse in the country under different names at different times – the national question, enthronement of true federalism, resource control, zoning etc?

It is important to underline that calls for a sovereign national conference have always had both political and economic undertones. Politically the calls reflect an implicit recognition that virtually all the constituent units of the federation feel dissatisfied with the Nigerian arrangement and believe that they are either short-changed or will fair better under a different structure. In fact, every unit of the federation has a scar to convince the others that it is indeed being 'marginalised'. In this sense, the SNC is often a euphemism for a clarion call for the constituents of the federation to come together to renegotiate the basis of their 'marriage of convenience', including what would be the appropriate number of states for the federation and the way each unit should be made to feel that it is a real stakeholder in the Nigeria project.

Yes, among the proponents of the SNC are those who believe that everyone will be better off with a peaceful divorce (Adibe, 2011a).

The calls for a SNC are equally economic-driven. Over and above the concerns of the ethno-regional forces are issues about the appropriate revenue-sharing formula not only among the states but also between the centre and the states.

Despite the fact that our constitution is almost exclusively consumption-oriented – spelling out who gets what, when, and how (but largely silent on how the national cake should be baked or expanded), the issue of sharing the 'national cake', including power at the centre, remains one of the most divisive issues in our political history.

There is no doubt that the issues that the SNC seeks to resolve are crucial and vital – and must be confronted honestly and decisively if we genuinely hope to fashion out a nation out of the mosaic of nationalities that make up the Nigerian state. What is however unclear is whether the SNC is the best vehicle for resolving those vital issues. There are indeed several sources of concern: apart from the elected representatives, who should be invited to such a Conference? What should be their claim for being the authentic spokespeople of the constituencies they purport to represent? Wouldn't SNC exacerbate the very problems they are meant to resolve as many of the conferees are likely to see the platform as an opportunity for grandstanding? Throw onto these the ethnic profiling and name calling that usually follow such conversations in the media and one wonders whether SNC might not be the last straw that could push the country, ever on the precipice, onto the abyss. Even more worrying is the Republic of Benin scenario being played out.

It should be recalled that when President Matthew Kerekou was forced to convene the National Conference of Active Forces on February 19 1990 (the events that led to this were triggered by student protest in January 1989), the 488 conferees soon declared themselves sovereign, suspended the republic's constitution, dissolved the national assembly and created the post of prime minister (Koko, 2008). This likely scenario is one of the reasons why no government of the day at the centre is likely to be a fervent supporter of a SNC.

It would also seem that SNC has become one of the tools in the games played by the various ethnic and regional factions of the Nigerian elite. For instance when the Northern faction of the Nigerian elite move their 'game' of population - i.e. calls that emphasize the use of population in which the North has an advantage - in the allocation of privileges or Sharia law as happened under the first term of Obasanjo's presidency (1999-2003), the calls for SNC, and 'resource control' would usually get more strident. In these hide-and-seek games, the SNC is most closely associated with the South-west faction of the Nigerian elite while 'resource control' is thought to be the joker in the arsenal of the South-South faction of these elite.

It is remarkable that even the states in the South which stand to lose even more than the North if there were full 'resource control' (meaning people from Niger Delta keeping all the proceeds from the oil found in their area), often support the call for resource control – a clear indication that such calls often have serious political undertones (Adibe, 2012).

Given the real potential that the SNC could exacerbate the problem it is meant to resolve through the likely grandstanding and trading of blames that would dominate the proceedings (apart from the problem of how to choose the various representatives and the issue of how to delineate what truly constitutes the 'federating units in the country), it may be better for the various political parties to be encouraged to articulate their positions on some of the issues the SNC proposes to resolve and then use such as part of their bases for canvassing for support. This could then become a basis for distinguishing one party from the other. This is why the PDP's zoning arrangement – as imperfect as it is and as pedestrian as the party has been in governing the country in many respects – appears to be a major effort in this direction (Adibe, 2011b).

It is true the above option could give rise to regional parties with separatist tendencies but there is nothing wrong with this because once the parties are drawn into canvassing for support for their ideas, the shine and glamour will most likely be taken off some of those ideas. This is why in many mature democracies even right wing parties are allowed to exist and to canvass for support because of fears that outlawing them or not allowing them to freely subject their ideas in the competition of marketplace of political ideas could glamourise such ideas.

There is no need to insist that all political parties must be national parties – there should be space for regional parties and for parties that espouse single causes – such as the Green parties that are very closely associated with environmental issues. In this scenario and since it appears that people's votes are beginning to count in this country, the ultimate decision on which direction the country should go will then be left directly for the citizens to decide rather than self-serving conferees under a SNC.

There is often an erroneous assumption that once the problems of inter-ethnic and inter-regional relations are resolved, the 'national question' will also have been resolved. The truth is that the contentious issues that play out at the national level also find expressions at the regional and state levels. In some states or geopolitical zones for instance, the contradictions among the various sub-national, sub-ethnic and special interests are more virulent than you find at the national level.

This is why we feel it may be necessary at both the national and state levels, to have bicameral legislatures, with one chamber emphasising the equality of states or local governments (at the state level) and the other chamber, with about 50 percent of the members appointed, aggregating the various special interests and contending forces. The two chambers should serve as checks and balances to ensure that vital and special interests are taken into considerations in making laws that affect the country or the state – or the geopolitical zones if they become the units for allocating privileges.

In addition to using political parties to aggregate the contending interests and visions of the direction the country should go, we will also recommend the following as a way of resolving the severe crisis in the country's nation-building project:

Since we have argued that Boko Haram is a reflection of the crisis in the country's nation-building and that Sovereign National Conference could worsen the problem, in addition to allowing political parties to aggregate these contentious interests as discussed above, there are other creative ways rebuilding trust not only among the constituent units of the federation but also trust in the government. We recommend the following:

The structure of the country

We believe that the greatest challenge the country has today is not poverty and underdevelopment but politics. Our nation-building is without doubt in deep crisis. At the heart of this crisis is the distribution of political and economic privileges.

We will recommend that the six geopolitical zones should replace the States and Local Governments as the units for sharing these privileges. The government of each of the six geo-political zones will be constitutionally empowered to determine whether it wants to have a bicameral legislature or not, the number of States and local governments it wants to have and which units within its boundary (States, Local Governments or Town Unions) will be used in sharing its own revenues and on which formula. We also favour granting such each geopolitical zone the power to have its own police.

There are several advantages in using the six geopolitical zones as units for sharing economic and political privileges: First, it will automatically reduce the size of government at the centre because only six zones rather than 36 States will be used in ensuring that the federal character is reflected

115

in the appointment of Ministers and top officials of the public service. Second, since the zones are sufficiently large, it will moderate the pull of the centrifugal forces by moving substantially the site of the contest from the centre to the geopolitical zones, which are likely to have challenging internal contradictions. Third, making the geopolitical zones the only units that share resources and privileges with the federal government will be a very close approximation to what some people call 'true federalism'. Fourth, the perpetual cries of marginalisation by virtually all the units of the federation, which have contributed in undermining the country's nation-building project, will become muffled. We do not think there should be any fear that any geopolitical zone may one day break away from the federation because the internal contradictions in each zone will be a sufficient bulwark against such.

Formula for sharing revenue

We will recommend a sharing formula of 40 percent for the federal government, 50 percent for the six geopolitical zones and 10 percent as ecological and natural disaster fund (for fighting erosion, desert encroachment, oil spill etc). There should however be more effective control of the Governors because at present both the legislature and the judiciary at the state level appear to be in the pocket of the Governors. There is an urgent need to find means of reducing the power of the Governors through more effective checks and balances.

Zoning to unzone

It was the late K.O. Mbadiwe who coined the phrase, 'zoning to unzone'. By this we believe the 'man of timber and calibre' was merely saying it was a way of giving each part of the country the proverbial sense of belonging in the Nigeria project. From all indications the issues raised by the PDP's zoning and power rotation arrangements during the party's acrimonious presidential primaries in 2010 are far from being fully resolved. At that time the anti-zoning lobby advanced several arguments why zoning and power rotation arrangements were either not

117

good for the country or should not be a hindrance to Jonathan contesting the election. The zoning proponents too had their own arguments. In the end Jonathan contested and won.

In theory that would have resolved the zoning controversy. But going by the fallouts from the media reports of the PDP's zoning formula for the principal offices of the National Assembly, it seems that the issue will for a long time continue to generate controversies especially whenever a new government is to be instituted. PDP members of the House of Representatives went against the party's recommended zoning formula and chose the leadership of the House that they wanted. When it suits them, previously anti-zoning elements turn into proponents of zoning and power rotation while proponents of zoning often pick-and choose - when zoning and power rotation should be applied or not. So why do many Nigerians seem to flip-flop on the zoning issue? There are several salient issues here:

It will appear that many people instinctively recognise the benefits of zoning but at the same time do not want a rigid application of the principle - perhaps in order not to ossify the political process. This approach-avoidance attitude, including by some PDP stalwarts, has created regrettable fuzziness around the issue, especially on conditions under which it should be strictly applied and when it should be discarded.

Former President Olusegun Obasanjo has for instance taken at least four stances on the issue - first he denied that zoning existed in the party's constitution and then shifted into an obscurantist 'when you are there you are there and when you are not there, you are not there'(Adibe, 2011b). Obasanjo had also, at different times, argued that zoning was suspended to enable Jonathan run for the presidency and equally contradictorily held that the party's zoning arrangement was still very much alive. He has also continued to insist that the present Speaker of the House should vacate so that the slot would be taken by someone from the Sout-west where his party had zoned the post.

Obasanjo is not alone in flip-flopping over zoning. In Imo Sate for instance, there was reportedly a zoning arrangement among the three senatorial zones in the area when it comes to producing the State Governor. Under this arrangement, the Okigwe senatorial district (where former Governor Ikedi Ohakim comes from) was expected to produce the Governor until 2015. However in the last Governorship election in the state, it would seem that the electorate favoured a dispensation for Rochas Okorocha who actually comes from Orlu Senatorial district – where Ohakim's predecessor in office Achike Udenwa hails from.

Again if reports in the media were anything to go by, most serving and newly elected members of the Senate wanted David Mark to retain the Senate Presidency. A strict application of the PDP's zoning and power rotation arrangements would have meant the office would be zoned to the South because

120

under the Obasanjo presidency, (from the South West), the post was also zoned to the South (South East) while under the Yaradua presidency (North West) it was zoned to the North (North Central). This presupposes a tradition of zoning the Senate presidency to the North if the president is from there or the South if the president is from the South. These instances show that both the zoning proponents and the anti-zoning elements during the acrimonious contest for the PDP presidential primary have sufficient grounds to claim vindication. Which, of course, only compounds the problem.

Not resolving the issue of the conditions under which the zoning and power rotation would be strictly applied and when they could be dispensed creates uncertainty such that any reconfiguration becomes vulnerable to suspicion, manipulation or being unduly politicised - some of the reasons why the zoning arrangement was put in place in the first instance.

We will argue that despite the obvious imperfections of zoning and power rotation

121

arrangements, in a multi-ethnic country like ours, where the constituent units deeply distrust one another, the certainty that a zone would occupy a certain position at a defined political moment could help to muffle cries of marginalisation and by so doing, remove a major clog in the nation-building process. In essence, what seems to be lacking is not so much whether there are circumstances in which zoning could be dispensed but how to compensate for the certainty that zoning and power rotation arrangements offer. True, that someone from one's ethnic group/geopolitical zone occupies a certain office does not necessarily guarantee progress for such a zone/ ethnic group. Unfortunately we have across the country a group of 'ethnic watchers' who have the capacity to press the right emotional button to throw a regime into a legitimacy crisis.

Another danger in not resolving the issue of zoning and when it should be rigidly applied or discarded is the danger of reviving the 'cluster politics' of the First and Second Republics where each major ethnic group formed a party it dominated with the hope of using the control of its enclave as a bargaining chip. The recent sweeping victory of the ACN in the South West in fact raises the possibility of a 'me-tooist' scenario. 'Cluster politics' should be regarded as a step backward in our nation-building process.

Related to the above is the emerging tendency for groups that exert an 'overwhelming claim' to a certain entitlement to be pacified with juicy political offices. This trend appears to have started with the annulment of the June 12 election won by the late Moshood Abiola. The danger is that without delineating a clear and predictable system of giving constituent units of the Nigerian federation assurances that they are real stakeholders in the Nigeria project, there could be tactical nurturing of militants and purveyors of violence to help groups stake 'overwhelming claims' to an entitlement.

Hate Crime legislation

Many countries have hate crime legislations, which criminalize hate speech on the basis of race, gender, religion, immigration status, and sexual orientation. On several occasions in recent years, the French government has fined actress Brigitte Bardot for hate speech directed against Muslims, immigrants, and those of mixed racial ancestry. In the UK for instance, if the police find out that a crime or verbal abuse is motivated by racial, gender or sexual orientation hatred, they will treat the incident very seriously and any sentence will be more severe than one for a similar crime without hate motive.

While there is very little one can do to stop people from having stereotypes, verbalizing such should be criminalized. Because people are not punished in this country for hate crime, people often freely and openly rain abuses on others' ethnicity, religion or even gender. It is time people were made to understand that such could lead to fines or even imprisonment.

Good leadership

Nigeria is in dire need of a Nyerere or Mandela - an honest, forward-looking father figure who will command legitimacy and respect across the major fault lines and who will genuinely place the country above self and his/her primordial identities. Nigeria can work but it needs re-building to meet the aspirations of the peoples and entities that make up the country. It is only through a conscious re-engineering that the crisis in the country's nation-building will be resolved, whichwill in turn halt the current rapid de-Nigerianisation process.

References

Kawu, Is'haq Modibbo (2012) 'Back to the sovereign national conference trenches' , Vanguard February 9, http://www.vanguardngr.com/2012/02/back-to-the-sovereign-national-conference-trenches/ (Accessed August 1, 2012)

Adibe, Jideofor (2012) 'The North, Revenue Allocation and the Games they Play', Daily Trust, March 8, (back page)

Adibe, Jideofor (2011a): 'Beyond a Sovereign National Conference' *Daily Trust*, June 2 (back page)

Adibe, Jideofor (2011b): 'Zoning: the Fire Next Time' *Daily Trust*, June 2 (back page) May 19

Index

A

Adibe, Jideofor, 23, 25, 27, 36, 64, 85, 95, 99, 101

Afghanistan, 30, 35, 69, 70

Al Qaeda in the Islamic Maghreb, 70, 71

Al Quaeda, 69, 74, 76

Al Shabaab, 71, 103

Alonge, Adebayo, 32, 33, 38, 59

Anderson, Benedict, 12, 13, 25

Arendt, Hannah, 99

Arewa People's Congress, 84

B

Bauchi, 37, 91

Bayelsa State House of Assembly, 87

Berlin Conference of 1884-1885, 9

Borno, 27, 36, 37

by Kanuri Muslims, 43

C

Campbell, John, 73

Chomsky, Noam, 49

Chukwumerije, Uche, 63

Constitution Drafting Committee, 18

Crisis State Research Centre, 50

D

Dala Alemderi Ward, Maiduguri, 27, 36

de-Nigerianisation, 24, 98, 100
Diiigbo, Goodluck, 87

E

Elaigwu, Isawa, 14, 16, 26

F

Failed State Index, 46, 47, 48, 49, 50, 51, 55
Fanon, Franz, 58
Federal Character Commission, 19, 26
for Ogoni people, 87

G

Gurr, Ted, 59, 60

H

Hate Crime legislation, 121
Horn of Africa, 50

I

Igbo nation, 12
Ijaw ethnic group, 67

K

Kanem-Bornu Empire, 43
Kano, 28, 37, 45
Katsina, 37

L

London School of Economics, 50

M

Maitatsine riots, 45
Mantzikos, Ioannis, 29, 30, 73
Maslow, Abraham, 56, 57
MASSOB, 64, 84
Mbadiwe, K.O., 115
MEND, 64, 84
Mohammed, Murtala, 18, 34, 36, 38, 39

128

N

NADECO, 64, 68
National Party of
Nigeria, 23
National Youth
Service Corp
scheme, 20, 90
Ndume, Ali, 39
Niger Delta, 58, 63,
86, 89, 102

O

Obasanjo, Olusegun,
23, 63, 85, 95, 96,
117, 118
Okorocha, Rochas,
118
Oodua Peoples'
Congress, 63

R

Royal Niger
Company, 10

S

Salafis, 31

Sanusi, Lamido
Sanusi, 30, 62, 86
Shekau, Abubakar, 36,
39, 68, 71
Sheriff, Ali-Modu, 38,
39
Shonekan, Ernest, 23
Sokoto, 37, 44
Sokoto Caliphate, 44
Somalia, 103

U

Udenwa, Achike, 118
UN building, Abuja,
69

W

Washington DC, 46
Wheare, K.C., 17, 26

Y

Yaradua, Umaru, 23,
65, 96, 118
Yobe, 35, 37
Yoruba nation, 12
Yusuffiya, 35

129

Z

Zoning, 22, 95, 115